Marie Antoinette

Katie Daynes

Illustrated by Nilesh Mistry

History consultant: Dr. Anne Millard

Edited by Lesley Sims
Designed by Russell Punter

First published in 2005 by Usborne Publishing Ltd.,
Usborne House, 83-85 Saffron Hill, London
EC1N 8RT, England.
www.usborne.com

Printed in Spain. UE.
First published in America in 2005.

Contents

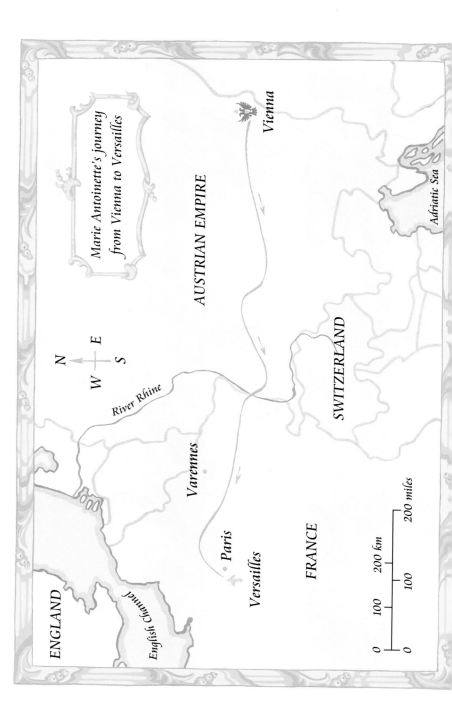

Chapter 1

Little Antoine

"It's been snowing all night!" cried Antoine, the youngest Archduchess of Austria, as she pulled back the heavy, embroidered curtains.

"Let's throw some snowballs before breakfast," said her sister Charlotte, excitedly. "Mother's meeting a Spanish diplomat this morning. She won't even notice we've gone."

They quickly dressed in warm furs and ran down the castle stairs.

The sisters were inseparable. Their real names were Maria Carolina and Marie Antoinette, but everyone called them Charlotte and Antoine. They spent their days dancing, playing music and racing around the gardens of their three royal castles.

Their only worry was pleasing their mother, Empress Maria Theresa. Luckily, with four sons, seven daughters and an empire to run, the Empress had little time to spare. They only really saw her at dinners and concerts, when they had to dress tidily and behave like adults.

Musicians came from all over Europe to entertain the Austrian royal family.

"Who's playing tonight?" Antoine asked her governess, early one morning.

"His name is Mozart," replied the governess, "and he's a child genius!"

When Mozart arrived, the sisters
stifled a giggle. He was only six, the
same age as Antoine. But as soon as his
fingers touched the keyboard, the girls
were spellbound.

"Bravo!" cried their father, Emperor
Francis, when Mozart finished. The
young boy jumped up, bowed, ran to
the Empress and sat on her lap. It was
such a funny sight, Antoine and
Charlotte couldn't help giggling again.

When the Empress wasn't listening to music or working, she was busy arranging marriages for her children.

"I think Mother's found another wife for Joseph," whispered Charlotte, one afternoon in the garden. Joseph was their eldest brother and heir to the Austrian Empire. The whole family had been upset when his first wife died giving birth to a daughter.

"Why would he want to get married again?" asked Antoine.

"Well, Mother says he needs a son..."

The two girls loved discussing other people's lives. One day, they would have to marry as well, but that seemed a long way off. Besides, their older sisters would need husbands first.

Joseph's second wedding was a magnificent occasion. The composer

Gluck had written a musical specially, with parts for Antoine's older brothers and sisters. When the applause died down, the younger children came on stage to dance in a ballet about love.

Antoine held a crook and played the role of a shepherdess. She stood very straight and kept her chin raised, just as her dance teacher had taught her.

Fortunately for Antoine, dancing, music and embroidery – the things she liked most – were crucial to a royal upbringing.

"If you can dance, sing and sew," said her governess, "you are sure to impress your future husband."

Antoine loved her governess. She was a kind and gentle teacher. And she knew Antoine struggled with reading and writing so she made those lessons extra short. But one morning the governess appeared very nervous.

"The Empress wants to see some of your writing," she said. "So... I've... er... written some words on a page. You just need to trace over them."

Relief swept over Antoine's face. Even tracing was hard work, but at least it would keep her mother happy.

The first of Antoine's sisters to marry and move away was Marie Christine, known at home as Mimi. She was a bossy, annoying older sister, and Charlotte and Antoine were glad to see her go. But their mother was in tears. Mimi was her dearest daughter and she would miss her deeply.

"Our governess says Mother let Mimi marry for love," whispered Charlotte, as they watched Mimi drive away. "She says Mother married for love too!"

The following
year, Antoine's
father died
suddenly,
plunging the
royal family
into mourning.
The Empress was
inconsolable. She
immersed herself in work for her
empire and wore nothing but black for
the rest of her life.

For Antoine, now eleven, life was
about to get worse. Her sister Josepha
was due to marry Ferdinand of Naples,
the King of Spain's son. The deal was
already signed and sealed when
Josepha caught smallpox and died.

Amidst the shock and sadness,
Charlotte burst into Antoine's room.

"I can't bear it!" she cried, tears staining her cheeks. "Mother said the King of Spain could choose another bride for his son, and he's chosen *me*!"

Antoine stared at her sister in horror. She hated being away from her beloved Charlotte for even a day. Now fate and their mother's ambitious plans were to separate the two sisters, maybe forever.

Chapter 2

Wedding preparations

Antoine passed the lonely days that followed playing her harp and stitching ornate patterns. When her gentle governess was replaced with a much stricter teacher, Antoine grew sadder still.

What worried her most was her mother's sudden interest in all that she did. How she dressed, how she walked, how she wore her hair... every detail was scrutinized.

"We really must sort out your crooked teeth," announced the Empress, soon after Antoine's twelfth birthday. "And your uneven hairline."

For three months, Antoine had to wear metal wires around her teeth. Then a French hairdresser was summoned to do her hair.

"Well, it's an improvement," said the Empress, curtly. "We'll get Ducreux to paint your portrait and dazzle the French court with your beauty. Then the King of France is sure to choose you as a bride for his grandson."

Antoine was horrified. So that's what her mother had been plotting. Suddenly everything made sense. Antoine had noticed the French Ambassador sitting next to the Empress at functions, but she didn't know they'd been discussing *her*.

Antoine thought about her other sisters. Marianne, the eldest, was disabled and would never marry. Poor Elizabeth hadn't left the castle since her pretty face had been scarred by smallpox. Amalia and Charlotte had been forced to marry last year. "That leaves only me," she sighed.

"My dear Charlotte," wrote Antoine that evening. "I've just found out that Mother wants me to marry a French prince named Louis. When his grandfather dies, he'll become King of France. That would make me Queen. I should be excited but I'm scared. Tell me that marriage isn't too awful..."

The next day, Antoine had to sit for hours in front of Ducreux and his easel. Finally, the Empress approved the portrait of her youngest daughter and it was sent with the Ambassador to the Palace of Versailles in France.

In the months that followed, Antoine had French language and history lessons every day. Her tutor – a priest named Vermond – was very kind and patient, but Antoine found it impossible to concentrate.

She much preferred galloping on horseback through the royal woodlands.

"Antoine!" the Empress cried, a fearful scowl on her face. "Future queens don't ride like stampeding cattle! They sit sidesaddle and trot along daintily."

"I'm not allowed to do anything fun anymore," thought Antoine, furiously.

The Empress was determined to make her daughter grow up quickly. On visits to the opera, Antoine now had to sit at the front of the royal box.

Members of the audience would crane their necks just to catch a glimpse of the Archduchess.

"There's the future Queen of France!" they whispered from row to row.

When Antoine arrived at a ball or official reception, there was a dramatic hush. All heads turned to watch her walk in. Foreign diplomats were enchanted by her grace and style, and young ladies even tried to copy her intricate French hairstyles.

The excitement began to rub off on Antoine. For each occasion, she had a wonderful new outfit to wear, with jewels to match. And, to her surprise, even her mother treated her kindly.

"You will make your people very proud," said the Empress. "Obey your husband and follow French customs, but never forget you're Austrian."

As Antoine grew more excited about her approaching marriage, she tried desperately to imagine what her future husband would look like. Eventually, a painting of Louis arrived... but it showed the young prince tilling a muddy field.

"There must be some mistake!" Antoine exclaimed.

Her tutor Vermond laughed. "It's supposed to show Louis's commitment to his country," he explained.

"Oh dear," sighed Antoine. "It will take me ages to understand the French." But she didn't have ages. Her marriage was only a month away.

According to royal custom, Antoine had to be married officially before she left for France. Her husband-to-be wouldn't be there, so one of her brothers had to stand in for him.

Leading up to the wedding, there was a week of dancing and feasting, including a vast supper party at her brother Joseph's palace. Then the ceremony took place in the beautiful church where Antoine's parents had been married.

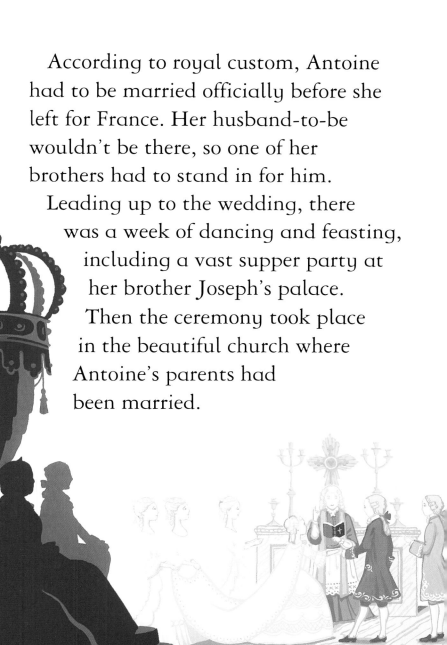

Two days later, fifty-seven carriages lined up outside the royal castle. Antoine hadn't slept all night. Today she would be leaving her family, her home and everything she knew for a new life at the lavish French court.

Outside in the cold spring air, the Empress hugged her daughter tenderly. "Do so much good to the French people," she said, "that they can say I've sent them an angel."

Then the stern Empress broke down in tears.

A gold and velvet carriage stood waiting for Antoine. Reluctantly, she left her mother and stepped on board.

As the procession snaked away from the castle, Antoine's sobs became uncontrollable. She leaned out of the carriage to catch every last glimpse of her mother and her past. From now on, she was Marie Antoinette, the future Queen of France.

Chapter 3

Meet your husband

The journey to the French border took two and a half weeks. At each village along the way, crowds rushed out to greet the procession and gawp at Marie Antoinette. For eight hours a day, she was cooped up in her carriage and each evening she had to attend an official meal. She was exhausted. Finally, the procession reached the river Rhine – the French border and the point of no return.

Marie Antoinette's carriage crossed a wooden bridge onto an island in the river, where a mini wooden castle had been built especially for her. She was shown into a dressing room and made to change from her Austrian clothes into a fashionable French dress of shimmering gold.

Her heart beat faster as she entered the next room, for at the far end stood a welcoming party from France. Marie Antoinette said a sad farewell to her travel companions and took her first few steps into France.

After speeches and formal introductions, she glanced behind her. The Austrians were gone. But there was no time for tears. Her journey continued on French soil, along roads edged with garlands, tapestries and cheering French peasants.

The next stop was the most nerve-wracking yet. Marie Antoinette had to meet the King of France and his grandson. As her carriage rattled to a halt, she couldn't bear the wait any longer. She jumped out, ran up to the figures waiting for her and made a low curtsey.

"I'm delighted to meet you," announced the King, taking her little hand and kissing it. "Let me introduce you to your husband, Louis, the Dauphin of France."

Marie Antoinette had been taught the word Dauphin. It meant "heir to the throne" in French. And she was now the Dauphine, the future Queen.

For the first time, the Dauphin and Dauphine faced each other. Young Louis seemed painfully shy but, after a nudge from his grandfather, he gave his new wife a quick peck on the cheek.

"And these are my daughters, Louis's aunts," said the King, indicating three fierce-looking princesses.

"Lovely to meet you," said Marie Antoinette in French, with a thick Austrian accent.

She soon forgot her nerves and chattered cheerfully as the King's carriage rumbled on. The King smiled at his charming new granddaughter, the aunts frowned in faint disapproval and the Dauphin stared sullenly at the carriage floor.

After a lavish meal and a night in a French castle, Marie Antoinette

was finally driven to her new home —
the Palace of Versailles. She looked out
of the carriage window, amazed. The
gardens and lakes seemed to stretch for
miles and the palace itself was far
grander than any Austrian castle.

Her first day at Versailles was also
her French wedding day. It took three
hours of fussing to dress the new
Dauphine. Then she had to smile and
look beautiful all afternoon, in front of
crowds of fascinated onlookers. She was
paraded through the dazzling Hall of
Mirrors and led to the royal chapel,
where her husband was waiting.

After the King and the Dauphin had signed the marriage certificate, Marie Antoinette's trembling fingers picked up the pen. Still not used to her new name, she almost forgot to add "tte" on the end. Then the ink smudged, leaving an embarrassing black blot.

Marie Antoinette

That evening, the royal family feasted in full view of nosy palace courtiers. Marie Antoinette was so overwhelmed, she couldn't eat a thing. By contrast, chubby Louis ate enough for two.

There was great excitement as the newlyweds left the table and were guided to their bedroom.

"Why is everyone following us?" whispered Marie Antoinette.

No one had warned her of the old French tradition, where servants gather to pay their respects to a royal couple on their wedding night. Only once the last maid had curtseyed and left were the Dauphin and Dauphine finally alone together.

Chapter 4

Life at Versailles

The first weeks at Versailles were a bewildering blur for Marie Antoinette. She was waited on throughout the day and not even allowed to wash or dress herself. Each morning, after breakfast and a visit to the royal aunts, maids spent an hour doing her hair. Then, at noon, her doors were opened to the public. Streams of people would elbow their way in to watch her make up her face.

Mealtimes were a public event too.
Anyone could enter the palace and
watch the royal family eat, so long as
they dressed well and the men carried
swords. Marie Antoinette found it all
very tiring. She was only fifteen and
wasn't used to adult company. She
much preferred playing with children
or walking her pet dog.

One adult she really disliked was the
Countess du Barry. She was the King's
lover. They weren't married, but that

didn't stop the King from laughing and flirting with her in public. The royal aunts were disgusted, and so was Marie Antoinette. "She's the most stupid and impertinent creature you can imagine," she wrote to her mother.

The Empress demanded a letter a month from her daughter. She wanted to know all the gossip from Versailles – in particular, how her daughter was getting along with her husband.

"Everything depends on the wife being obliging, gentle and amusing," wrote the Empress.

Marie Antoinette sighed. "But I try to be all those things," she thought, "and Louis *still* doesn't love me."

It was a whole year before the Dauphine found a true friend to confide in. She met the Princess de

Lamballe at a dance in the palace. The Princess reminded Marie Antoinette of her sister Charlotte and the two young ladies became very close.

"Louis spends all day hunting," the Dauphine sighed. "I see him at supper, where he eats like a horse, then he hides himself away in his room."

"He's dreadfully shy," said the Princess. "And he only became Dauphin because his older brother died. Perhaps you should take up riding, so you can spend more time with him?"

Before long, the Dauphine was riding after the royal hunt. When her mother found out, she was furious. "Riding will ruin your chances of bearing a son!" she wrote.

Marie Antoinette knew everyone wanted her to have a son – a future King for France. But her husband still seemed embarrassed just holding her hand. What more could she do?

Gradually, the situation improved. The royal couple had to make lots of public appearances together and Louis grew used to having a wife at his side.

That summer, they made their first official trip into Paris. It was a wonderful day. As they strolled through the Tuileries gardens, excited Parisians flocked around them. Even the Dauphin was smiling.

"How fortunate we are," Marie Antoinette later wrote to her mother, "to have gained the love of a whole people with such ease." No one told her about the real poverty and misery that faced most people in France.

She had been in France for four years when the King fell gravely ill. He had contracted the dreaded disease smallpox. Doctors crowded at his bedside, while Marie Antoinette and Louis waited anxiously for news.

All of a sudden, there was a clattering of footsteps. The King had taken his last breath and every courtier wanted to be the first to pay homage to their new rulers.

United in grief, King Louis and Queen Marie Antoinette knelt down and prayed.

Dear God, guide us and protect us. We are too young to reign.

Chapter 5

Queen of France

The new King and Queen spent the first six months of their reign away from Versailles and the highly contagious smallpox. On their return, Marie Antoinette had to get used to her new role. She was amazed to find she had five hundred people working just for her, from ladies-in-waiting and ministers to ushers and footmen.

"I'll never remember what they all do," she thought.

To her delight, becoming Queen seemed to make her even more popular with the French people. At a new opera by Gluck, the chorus chanted, "Let us sing, let us celebrate our Queen." Instantly, the audience turned and burst into applause. Watching from the royal box, Marie Antoinette wept with joy.

She was suddenly very popular in court too, but she found it hard to know who were real friends and who just wanted to be seen with the Queen.

Everyone expected their Queen to look stunning and Marie Antoinette didn't want to disappoint them. For Louis's coronation, she ordered a beautiful new dress, made by a French designer, Rose Bertin. It was very expensive, but what did money matter now she was Queen?

Little by little, Marie Antoinette became more confident at Versailles. She held lavish parties, put on shows for her friends and organized magnificent firework displays. With her mother hundreds of miles away, the only person she had to obey was her husband. As long as he agreed, she could do anything.

"I'd love to watch the dawn from our gardens," she told Louis one day.

"Then you shall," he replied, slightly bemused. "Just don't expect me to get out of bed."

Accompanied by countesses and courtiers, Marie Antoinette gazed in awe at the rising sun. "How romantic!" she sighed.

The journalists in Paris soon heard this story and rubbed their hands eagerly. Here was some gossip they could twist into a good story. They wrote a pamphlet, claiming the Queen had crept into the palace grounds at night and met with a secret lover.

Marie Antoinette just laughed at this ridiculous story. But soon more pamphlets were being circulated. The writers invented other lovers, mocked the Queen's extravagant clothes and hairstyles and, worst of all, insulted her for not producing an heir to the French throne.

"It's not fair," complained Marie Antoinette to her new best friend, the Countess de Polignac.

"The pamphlets are never fair," replied the elegant Countess.

Eight years into her marriage, at the age of twenty-two, Marie Antoinette finally received the wonderful news that she was pregnant. Everyone hoped it would be a boy, but that winter she gave birth to a girl.

Secretly, Marie Antoinette was pleased. A son and heir would become the property of France but a daughter was hers to love and keep. She dutifully named her child Marie Thérèse, a French version of her mother's name.

Soon after the birth, Marie Antoinette caught measles. "If I stay near the King, he might catch them too," she worried.

Fortunately, there was a little palace known as the Petit Trianon in the grounds of Versailles. The Queen could rest there until she'd recovered.

Marie Antoinette loved the Petit Trianon. It reminded her of her family's castle in the Austrian countryside. She spent three weeks there, going boating, taking walks and playing cards.

"The King is here," gasped the Princess de Lamballe one day. "He wants to see you!"

The Queen ran excitedly to the window. In the courtyard, safe from contamination, stood her husband.

"I miss you," he called up to her.

"I'll be home soon," she promised.

The following year, Marie Antoinette received the devastating news that her mother had died. They hadn't seen each other for almost ten years, but the Empress's regular letters had kept her in touch with Austria. Suddenly, Marie Antoinette felt cut off from her homeland and her past.

She was still grieving when she discovered she was pregnant again. At the birth, Louis sat nervously by his wife's bedside. He watched as the crying baby was taken away and took his wife's slender hand in his.

"You have fulfilled our wishes and those of France," he said solemnly. "You are the mother of a Dauphin."

Marie Antoinette gave a weak smile of relief. "If only my mother could have lived to see this day," she thought.

46

Chapter 6

Money trouble

While King Louis busied himself with meetings and paperwork, Marie Antoinette spent more and more time at the Petit Trianon. She had commissioned an exciting project in the palace grounds – the construction of a model village, complete with cottages, dovecotes, a windmill and a dairy. Then cows, sheep, hens and a goat were added, to recreate a pretty scene from the French countryside.

"We'll hold country dances here,"
cried Marie Antoinette, clapping her
hands in delight. In her model village
she felt much closer to the ordinary
French people. She had no idea how
poor they really were.

The pamphlet writers were quick to
report on Marie Antoinette's fancy
project. They portrayed her as a
frivolous, thoughtless foreigner and
blamed the country's high taxes on her
extravagant spending.

In truth, the Queen was becoming less extravagant. She found out that France had spent lots of money supporting the revolution in America and was careful only to buy two new dresses a week. When offered an elaborate, diamond necklace, she politely refused. Before long, a letter arrived thanking her for the purchase and asking for payment.

"But I didn't buy the necklace!" cried Marie Antoinette in surprise.

She soon discovered she was the victim of an evil hoax. A trickster, Jeanne de Lamotte, had forged Marie Antoinette's signature and taken the necklace herself. Then she'd left for England, where she could get a good price for the diamonds, leaving the Queen to pay the bill.

When the journalists reported this story, they portrayed the Queen as a lying thief, not an innocent victim. Poor Marie Antoinette felt hurt and mistreated. Worse still, most people believed what they read in the gossipy pamphlets.

By now, Marie Antoinette was thirty and had two more children, Louis Charles and baby Sophie.

"I'll show the French people that I'm the Mother of France," she decided, "and they will love me once more."

She commissioned a portrait of herself and her four children, to hang proudly in the palace of Versailles. But as the paint was still drying, little Sophie died. Marie Antoinette was distraught and quickly ordered the artist to paint out her baby.

Far from respecting the Queen as a mother, the French started jeering when she appeared in public.

"They're blaming me for their own problems," sighed Marie Antoinette, "but I've never done anything to harm them." She decided to find out what was really going wrong and began to attend her husband's meetings.

The Queen was shocked to hear that
France was almost bankrupt.

"We must raise more money by
increasing the peasants' taxes," said
one adviser.

"But they are already paying more
than they can afford," said another.

"Then we must get the noblemen and
priests to pay taxes too," announced
the controller of finance.

There was a hushed silence. The priests and noblemen were powerful men. They would never agree to paying taxes.

"We'll have to hold a meeting of the Estates," said the King, reluctantly.

"What are the Estates?" asked Marie Antoinette, after the meeting.

"Three groups representing the French people," explained Louis. "Priests make up the First Estate, noblemen the Second and everyone else the Third. The Estates haven't met for over a century. But since the Third Estate is the largest and the poorest, I'm sure they'll vote for the rich to pay more."

Unfortunately, the Third Estate had other ideas. Inspired by the American Revolution, they saw this meeting as their chance to change France forever.

Chapter 7

Revolution

Nine months later, eleven hundred representatives of the Estates met at the Palace of Versailles. Marie Antoinette, dressed in a simple white satin dress, sat on a throne next to her husband. Fanning herself nervously, she tried to focus on the angry speeches but her mind kept drifting. Her oldest son was seriously ill. He had never been a strong child and now he was more frail than ever.

As more meetings and debates raged around the palace, Marie Antoinette sat by her son's bed. He died in the middle of the night, aged only seven.

The King and Queen were deep in mourning when the Third Estate announced it was now the National Assembly of France. The people of France had voted for a different system of government, where the King had less power and authority.

Marie Antoinette tried to keep a low profile. There was talk of violence and uprisings in Paris, but her priority was to spend more time with her two remaining children.

They were enjoying a quiet afternoon at the Petit Trianon when the King summoned them back to the palace.

"A mob of market women are marching on Versailles," he explained to his wife. "It's not safe here. You must leave with the children."

"But my place is by your side," she replied. "I will not leave you."

A crowd of angry women arrived at the palace gates, demanding to see the King. Their shouting continued into the night and by dawn they had stormed the palace.

The royal family was herded together. Any guard who tried to protect them was brutally killed.

"To Paris! To Paris!" cried the crowd.

Huddled into a carriage with her husband and children, Marie Antoinette held her head high. She wanted to retain some dignity on the long, humiliating journey to Paris. Around her, mocking women whooped and jeered. How different this was from her celebrated arrival in France.

Chapter 8

The guillotine

The royal carriage was driven to the Tuileries palace in Paris.

"Is this to be our prison or our home?" demanded Marie Antoinette.

The guards remained silent.

As weeks turned to months, the King and Queen tried to make the most of their new home. They resumed their familiar daily routine, had furniture and clothes delivered from Versailles and even held the occasional party.

With their fate so uncertain, Marie
Antoinette's main concern was her son,
Louis Charles, who was now the French
Dauphin. The safest option would be
to escape Paris with him, but she
refused to leave without her husband.
Only when the National Assembly
threatened to take the boy away did
the King agree to come too.

At the dead of night, the whole
family rode off in a large carriage,
with Louis Charles disguised as a
little girl. It was a daring move
and it almost worked...

...but the carriage was spotted by a guard in the small town of Varennes. Once more, the royal family was driven to the Tuileries palace.

By now, thousands of peasants were marching through the streets and no rich person was safe. The new leaders of France decided to move the King and Queen to a stronger prison... only just in time. That evening, a rabble of peasants swept through the Tuileries, looting royal possessions and massacring the King's guards.

Meanwhile, Marie Antoinette and her family were imprisoned in a guarded tower.

All day, revolutionary songs drifted over the walls, taunting the Queen in particular.

"Madame goes up into the tower," chanted the guards. "When will she come down again?"

In fact, the King was the first to leave the tower. He was put on trial for treason and attempting to desert his own people. The jury found him guilty. Excited cries from the street told Marie Antoinette of her husband's fate. He was to be executed by a deadly blow of the guillotine.

That night, the King said a brief farewell to his family before bravely facing his death. Marie Antoinette was numb with grief. She refused to eat or talk to anyone, not even her beloved children.

As her health deteriorated, the Queen was taken away to a dark, dingy prison cell. The French people were calling for her blood too. Denied even her embroidery, she spent the lonely days wondering what she'd done to deserve this.

Eventually, she was put on trial, accused of assisting the King in treason and also mistreating her son. The Queen was horrified. She loved her son more than herself. How could anyone make up such lies?

I appeal to all mothers who may be present...

After two days in the courtroom, the jury wrote down their verdict and asked the Queen to read it. Guilty. She was sentenced to follow her husband to the guillotine.

Marie Antoinette refused to show any emotion. Rejected as a queen, deprived of her husband and insulted as a mother, she no longer had a role to play in life.

The next morning, she boldly climbed the execution platform. Stopping only to apologize for stepping on a guard's toe, she lay her head under the guillotine blade and left the bloody revolution behind her.

My Royal Life

1755 – I was born in Vienna, Austria.

1765 – My father, Emperor Francis, dies.

1769 – My mother, Empress Maria Theresa, and King Louis XV of France decide I must marry his grandson.

1770 – I make the long journey to France.

1774 – Louis XV dies. My husband is suddenly King of France and I am his Queen.

1778 – Finally, I give birth to a child, Marie Thérèse.

1785 – I am accused of not paying for a diamond necklace, but I never even owned it. The people of France are beginning to hate me.

1789 – A mob of women storm Versailles and march me and my family to Paris in utter humiliation.

1791 – We flee Paris at night but are arrested in Varennes and forced back to the Tuileries.

1792 – We are imprisoned in the tower. Oh, the injustice.

1793 – My harmless, well-meaning husband is accused of treason and beheaded in front of his own people.

1794 – I too stand accused and must face my own death under the blade...

Let them eat cake!

The story goes... Marie Antoinette heard that the French peasants had no bread and replied, "Then let them eat cake." But this tale was being told about another princess in France before Marie Antoinette even arrived. It's very unlikely that she said it too.